It Happened to ME

Excluded

Interviews by Angela Neustatter and Helen Elliott
Photography by Laurence Cendrowicz

W

FRANKLIN WATTS
LONDON•SYDNEY

© 2003 Franklin Watts

First published in Great Britain by
Franklin Watts
96 Leonard Street
London
EC2A 4XD

Franklin Watts Australia
45-51 Huntley Street
Alexandria
NSW 2015

ISBN: 0 7496 4337 4

A CIP record for this book is available from the British Library.

Printed in Malaysia

Series editor: Sarah Peutrill
Art director: Jonathan Hair
Design: Steve Prosser
Photographs: Laurence Cendrowicz (unless otherwise credited)

Picture credits: Paul Baldesare/Photofusion: 26, 29, 32. Matt
Hammill: 34, 37, 38. Crispin Hughes/Photofusion: 42. Christa
Stadtler/Photofusion: 30. All Photofusion photographs posed by
models. Whilst every attempt has been made to clear copyright
should there be any inadvertent omission please apply in the first
instance to the publisher regarding rectification.

With grateful thanks to Trevor Philpott at C-Far (the Centre for
Adolescent Rehabilitation), Ken Claxton, founder of Youthbuild, and
all our interviewees.

Contents

Introduction

What is exclusion?

Exclusion - sometimes called 'being expelled' - is when a child is sent home from school as a punishment, or because he or she is thought to be unmanageable. Sometimes this is a temporary measure and may only last for a few days. At other times it will be permanent, and the child will have to attend a different school or find alternative education.

Who is at risk from exclusion?

The main causes of permanent exclusion are bullying, racism and violence. Exclusion rates vary greatly from school to school, but tend to be higher in poorer areas. Boys are more likely to be excluded, and it is especially common for children who live in care. The latter are often in and out of foster care or moving between parents, they frequently change schools, are unable to catch up or make friends, and start to play truant.

Many excluded children say their parents show little interest in homework and rarely attend parent-teacher evenings. They may also have a lack of role models.

What are its effects?

Exclusion can be very upsetting for everyone involved - teachers, child and family. Research shows that it often leads to serious problems such as taking drugs. It is also thought to be a key trigger leading to homelessness.

Exclusion often affects those most in need of education. Many excluded pupils don't get back into mainstream education, which is a heavy cost to both society and the individuals concerned.

Is exclusion necessary?

Although teachers, parents and children agree that, where possible, exclusion should be prevented, many schools find they need it as a measure that they can impose as a last resort - for example, when a student is putting other children's education or safety at risk. Gary, a headteacher, outlines the case for this on page 40. Sometimes it can be a positive thing - as Barney (page 26) and Mustapha (page 34) found out. However, without careful follow-up attention it is likely that problems will simply be passed on to other schools.

The following advice may be helpful if you, or someone you know, is facing exclusion.

What to do if you have been threatened with exclusion:

◆ Let your parents or carers know what is going on (the school should do this for you).
◆ Make sure you know why the exclusion has been threatened.
◆ Try to talk to your parents/carers or teachers about what has to change to ensure you can stay at your current school.

What to do if you have been temporarily excluded:

◆ Check when you can go back to school.
◆ When you return make sure you and your parents/carers know what's expected of you.

What to do if you have been permanently excluded:

◆ The organisations listed on page 46 can help you find out what to do next, based on your situation.

It Happened to Dawoud

DAWOUD was permanently excluded from school at the age of 15 for being disruptive and getting into fights. He now works for a building firm in Bradford, Yorkshire, where he lives.

Q What are your memories of young childhood?

A I grew up with my parents and my two younger sisters, younger brother and elder brother. But my father, a lorry driver, wasn't around much so Mum did most of the bringing up of us kids.

Q Did your parents feel strongly that you should get a good education?

A They did and they talked to me, even when I was young, about going to school and doing well and getting into college. I went to primary school at five and I enjoyed that. We did lots of creative things with paints and stuff and the

It's a Fact that...

Permanent exclusions happen to:
◆ 0.04 per cent of English primary school pupils,
◆ 0.34 per cent of secondary school pupils,
◆ 0.54 per cent of special school pupils.

teachers were nice. I did get into play fights with other children and I was ticked off by the headteacher, but never very seriously. I had lots of friends and my parents were quite happy with me.

Q So when did things change?

A I left when I was eight and went to middle school (there was a three-school system in Bradford at the time). The first year was all right. But then kids started on at me because I was much taller and bigger than anyone else. That upset me and, of course, I reacted. Because I was easily spotted I was often seen as the one causing trouble. One teacher used to jab his finger in my chest and shout at me. It made me very resentful of him.

Q How did that affect you?

A I began to dread going to school and I told my parents. My dad went and saw the teachers and things changed for a bit, but then it all started up again just the same. Some of the teachers were fair, but others just seemed to pick on me. I kept going to school, although I was sometimes late, until I was due to leave for secondary school.

Q Did you worry you would have problems at secondary school?

A Yes, I felt very nervous about going but I hoped it would get easier because all the kids would be bigger and I wouldn't stand out. But then, almost on my first day, another boy said to me he

thought I was the toughest there because of my size. That was how everyone seemed to see me. I was shoulder-bashed all the time by other children. At first I ignored it but then one day I retaliated and I punched the person who was shoulder- bashing me quite hard. I knew it would turn into a fight.

Q So were you blamed for that?

A I was and I was excluded for a couple of weeks. Then when I was back in school it just started up again. I tried telling teachers, but they wouldn't listen to me.

" ... kids started on at me because I was much taller and bigger than anyone else. "

7

> **"The headteacher just said it was up to me to deal with my problems in a non-violent way."**

The headteacher just said it was up to me to deal with my problems in a non-violent way.

Q Did your parents support you?

A My dad went into school again to ask the teachers what was going on. Then he told me not to get into trouble any more. I was really unhappy at school by this time, although I always went, and it was affecting my education. I'd fallen behind, particularly with reading. I did get offered some special needs teaching. I went a few times but I found it boring, so I stopped going. But nobody said anything. I was also answering back in class and then getting sent out, so I wasn't liked by the staff.

Q You were eventually permanently excluded from this school. Why?

A I was thrown out when I was 15. I was behind a hut in the school grounds, where people went for a smoke at break time, and this white lad appeared. He was making these bad racist comments and he wouldn't stop. I asked what was going on, and he said more things and then threw a punch at me, catching my shoulder. I just lost it then. I went for him in a rage. As I'm so large I pack a lot of strength and it ended up with him having a broken nose, jaw and rib. I was permanently excluded right away.

Q What happened then?

A I was charged with serious assault and taken to the police station. My parents were terribly upset. My father was in Pakistan, his home country, at the time and my mum, who comes from there, can't speak English so it was difficult for her to do anything. In fact the case didn't go ahead because the parents of the boy I had hurt were very decent. They came to my house with their solicitor and said they were dropping charges because, although he didn't deserve what I had done to him, they knew what he was like. And they didn't want me to go to prison.

It's a Fact that...

Bullying, fighting and assaults on peers account for around 30 per cent of exclusions in the UK.

Q Did your parents try to get you into another school?

A They were certainly upset at the idea that I had finished school but no, they didn't look for another place. I was out of education for about a year. I was on the streets during that time mixing with older boys who had left school and were into crime. We chilled out most of the time. We made money by buying things cheaply, like mobile phones, then selling them for more. Sometimes we'd get half an ounce of ganja [cannabis] and sell it for a profit. We spent it all on nights out drinking, going to clubs, that kind of thing. I didn't think at all about my future, or where all this might lead.

Q Didn't your parents get upset about this?

A They didn't know. When I left home in the mornings I told them I was looking for college placements. Sometimes I actually went into colleges and asked about courses so my parents could know this if they asked.

It's a Fact that...

In the UK about 8 per cent of permanently excluded children are Afro-Caribbean. Afro-Caribbean children make up about 1 per cent of the school population.

In New Zealand in 2001 Maori students made up 21 per cent of the school population but were involved in 47 per cent of exclusions.

Then a letter arrived from the local authority offering me a place at a special unit to work towards GCSEs. Dad opened the letter and he took me down there.

Q Were you willing to go back into education?

A I really didn't want to go, but I said I'd go once and have a look. When I got there I was surprised how different it was to school. The atmosphere was very relaxed and kindly and the teachers were friendly and informal so I decided I would try it. There were some kids with real problems, kids who couldn't control themselves, so we all had one-to-one teaching which I liked. In fact I took GCSE's after five

months and got D passes in science, maths, Urdu and geography. Then, when I finished, the head of my year called my dad in and said I should do sixth form. I didn't want to go back into an ordinary school again. I was 16 by then and I knew I was allowed to leave school.

Q Did you know what you wanted to do then?

A No I didn't. So I told my dad that I had signed on for college. That went on for about eight months. Letters started arriving from the careers office wanting to know what was happening because I wasn't going to college or signing on. I went along to the office and there was nothing suitable. But two months later they sent me off to see this organisation

called Youthbuild. They take on young people who are seen to need an opportunity. I was told later that if they had known about my fighting and the charge of assault they would not have taken me. You have to prove yourself to be taken on. They explained that I would be involved in building schemes.

Q Did you see it as an opportunity to make a career rather than going back to the street life?

A I wasn't sure and my first reaction was I'll give it a shot and leave if I don't like it. But I had wonderful training.

" I didn't think at all about my future, or where all this might lead."

" I think the teachers should have been more willing to listen to me and understand my problems. "

My manager really helped me see I was being given an opportunity to make something of my life. We did joinery and carpentry and I got an NVQ. We had lessons at college in practical building skills - things like putting on a roof - and it was all well taught. We learnt a lot of technical stuff and how to be a site foreman. And through doing this I learnt literacy because when I was stuck at reading something the lecturer went to a lot of trouble to explain and help me. When I could read I loved it and I started going to the library to research.

Q How did you get on with the other people?

A There were no personality clashes. I was the only black lad but that wasn't a problem - there was no racism.

Q How did your parents feel about the direction you had taken?

A I was living at home with them and they were very pleased and saw that as well as doing the training I was going to college.

Q Did this training lead to work?

A I was at college for six months before I was offered a placement on a building site for four days a week and one day in college. I got paid £45 a week, which wasn't much but I was an apprentice. After that Bradford Council offered me a job working on buildings for the local authority and I now earn a good wage.

It's a Fact that...

There is evidence to show a link between missing school and getting sucked into crime. One study shows: 5 per cent of all offences were committed by children during school hours; 40 per cent of robberies, 25 per cent of burglaries and 20 per cent of criminal damage were committed by 10-to 16-year-olds.

Q Looking back do you feel school failed you?

A I think the teachers should have been more willing to listen to me and understand my problems. If they'd done this and protected me more I might have got a proper education. I do feel upset that this was not how it happened. If I hadn't been lucky enough to get my chance with Youthbuild, life would have been a lot harder and I don't know how I would have coped. ■

Talking Points

◆ Dawoud thinks the school failed him. Do you agree? Is violent behaviour acceptable if it has been provoked?

◆ Youthbuild, the organisation that particularly helped Dawoud, would not have helped him if they had been aware of his school report. Do you think this is fair? Should exclusion records be permanently held?

It Happened to Greg

Greg 's mother was killed when he was three. His father turned to drink and Greg went to live with his grandmother. He was permanently excluded from primary school at the age of eight. After that he was taken into local authority care, had a series of different placements and ended up in prison. He now lives in North Devon.

Q Do you remember how you felt when your mum was killed?

A I remember life seemed to turn into chaos for me and my three older brothers. Family life didn't exist. Dad couldn't cope at all and he just cut off from the world and turned to drink. I suppose we would have been put into care then but my gran stepped in. She had a heart of gold and really tried to care for us although she had eight kids of her own to look after.

Q When did you start school?

A At five years old I went to primary school in Cheshire, but I never settled. I just knew things weren't all right at home because my dad had a temper and kept going off... once he got arrested for smashing up the house. He frightened us kids sometimes. The school sent letters to my dad saying I wasn't co-operating but of course he didn't take any notice. The teachers did try to help because they could see I was unhappy. They asked me what was wrong, but I didn't really understand myself so I couldn't tell them.

Q Were they able to help you settle in school?

A Not really. I was just upset all the time and my behaviour got worse. I was fighting, setting light to things, tipping tables over, throwing my dinner across the room. The school couldn't control me. So in the end they decided they had to exclude me.

Q Did you get any support from home?

A My gran tried hard to help me because she knew I was upset about my mum, but she had her own kids to care for too. A lot of the time I was just having to cope on my own. But then, after I was excluded, someone from the local authority came and took me to social services. I met this woman called Vera who gave me a foster placement. I didn't really understand what was going on - I assumed I would soon go home. But Vera was very good to me and she understood my troubles, so, although I missed my gran, I was happy to be there. I stayed three years

Q Did you go to school?

A Vera found a good school for me and I made some real friends. I went to lessons and found I enjoyed learning because the teachers helped me a lot. Everyone seemed happy with me. But then, when I was 11, I had an argument with Vera to do with my dad. He had turned up at Vera's - he wasn't supposed to do that. I was meant to see him once a week in a special place organised by the local authority, but sometimes he turned up drunk and fell all over the place. When I saw Dad that time I wanted to go with him. I ran away from Vera's and she wouldn't have me back.

Q So did you go to live at home with your dad?

A No. I wasn't allowed to. I was sent to a children's home, which was horrible. I was the youngest there and there were some very disturbed kids. I never made friends and I never felt safe. I was left alone in my room a lot and I became a loner. They knew I had to be educated. They tried to get me a private tutor as I was so much younger than

It's a Fact that...

Most excluded primary school children come from inner city schools and start secondary school with a reading age behind that of their peers.

15

others in the class but I didn't want that. Then they sent me to a boarding school in the Lake District. There were a lot of children my age there but because people were coming and going all the time it was hard making friends. The staff were kind and they did lots of activities with us.

Q So did you settle down?

A I didn't really. I thought a lot about my family. I felt there should be a home for me with them. When I was 13 I ran off and nicked a motorbike. I rode down the dual carriageway trying to get home but of course the police caught me. They sent me straight back to the school and that was when it kicked in that I'd never be with my family again.

> " ... because people were coming and going all the time it was hard making friends. "

It's a Fact that...

In the UK around 83 per cent of excluded pupils are boys. 80 per cent of exclusions are children between 12 and 15. However, exclusions at primary ages are rising fast – by 18 per cent in 1995-96.

Q How were you doing with education?

A I was about two years behind. I found learning difficult. The staff were kind and they tried to encourage and help me as much as possible. They pushed me as far as they could to get me to work. But I didn't see the point of education. I had to leave anyway when I was 14 because I was too old for the school and I was sent back to Cheshire.

Q Who did you live with there and did you go to school?

A I was placed with a couple who had three sons of their own and were very kind to me. The husband was a mechanic and he taught me about the inside of cars, which I

found interesting. I was close to home so I popped out often and went over to see my dad. We were able to say quite a lot of things to each other by then. It was good because I felt I was helping him. They sent me to a secondary school unit for children with special needs because I was about four years behind. I liked that. It was small, they had time for me and they really made me want to learn.

Q So things calmed down at this time?

A Well not really because I was heaving inside all the time, angry, crying myself to sleep sometimes. Dad stopped talking to me and I didn't know why. He had just cut me off. I was out a lot nicking motorbikes and breaking into houses. When I did these things I felt better because I had a sense of control over life. I was

" ... I didn't see the point of education."

17

also into solvent abuse - methane gas - and I went out to rob shops when I was high. I did it outside of school hours.

Q Did your foster family know?

A They did because I was getting arrested all the time. Eventually they said they couldn't keep me. I tried to understand, but all I really felt was worthless and disgusting - nobody wanted to keep me.

Q So how did you feel about yet another placement?

A Terrible. But then suddenly my dad told social services I could live with him. Although I was only 15 I went to live with him. Nobody bothered about me going to school again. Dad managed to get me a job in an engineering factory by getting documents saying I was 16. I got on well there and I actually got two NVQ passes. Unfortunately Dad got much worse and started to drink again. He went into a downward

spiral. I suppose I did too. By the time I was 17 I was getting into trouble with drugs: using cannabis and taking ecstasy, amphetamines and crack cocaine. When people said bad things - and people on drugs say lots of bad things - about my father, I'd burgle their homes and take their drugs and sell them. I got into a lot of fights. I was really at rock bottom.

Q Were you in danger?

A I was and I knew I had to move. I got on a bus to Torquay, although I had no money. I lived on the streets for a few weeks. It was then that I started doing burglaries seriously.

I got caught by the police this time. The judge sentenced me to two years in prison.

Q Did you feel that was the end of the line?

A In fact, although I didn't like prison, it gave me a breathing space to think about where my life was going. I was given some education and really caught up with some of the learning I'd missed. When I left prison I was offered the chance to do the C-Far [Centre for Adolescent Rehabilitation and Training] course where the people helped

me sort out my feelings a lot. They got me some fork-lift truck training and a home.

Q And what about your dad?

A He was devastated when I went to prison and felt he had failed me. So we were able to talk and things have improved with us. Things look better than they have for years. I look back to being excluded from school and think I could have had a happier childhood if that hadn't happened. I missed out on a lot, including being with my family in my own home. ∎

Talking Points

◆ Primary school exclusions, such as Greg's, are more unusual but they are increasing. Why do you think this is? Is it likely to be more damaging to be excluded from primary school? Or secondary school? What do you think?

◆ Governments believe that exclusion is bad for children and they endeavour to reduce the exclusion rates. However, where a child is as disruptive as Greg, it may be done to help the other children. Who should come first?

It Happened to Jessica

Jessica was excluded from a private school at the age of 14 for bad behaviour. At 17 she was excluded from a boarding school for drug-taking. She blames much of the wild behaviour that led to these exclusions on the lack of parenting when she was growing up, and her parents' divorce. She has now written a book and started workshops for teenagers going through problems when growing up.

Q What are your memories of growing up as a child?

A From day one I was pretty much brought up by nannies because both my parents worked in the family fashion and public relations business and they worked very long hours. It seemed as though we had thousands of nannies. Some stayed a while, others very briefly. They got me and my brother Josh up in the mornings, made breakfast, took us to school, collected us, gave us supper and put us to bed. Just Sundays and holidays were family days but even then the nanny always came along.

Q Did you mind about your parents being so busy?

A Having parents who were never there in the way other children's were made me feel different. I wanted them to be there more. A few times I think I attempted to ask my mother for more time. She was annoyed by that and said she was working for the family. I think my dad understood a bit better how I felt and he did stay at home more often.

Q So what happened with you at school during this time?

A I went to private schools. I was never interested in studying but I managed to get by without really trying. Every school report said, 'Jessica could do much better if she tried', and that I was lazy. My interest was in making friends and seeing how many rules I could break and get away with it.

Q Did you get into trouble with your parents?

A They worried about what was going on. They sent me to boarding school in my early teens. There my behaviour got really

> " My interest was in making friends and seeing how many rules I could break... "

It's a Fact that...

In Britain girls comprise just 17 per cent of permanent exclusions. As a consequence, girls have been largely overlooked in school exclusion prevention programmes and research. However, these recorded permanent exclusions are a small proportion of the total number of girls excluded. Many more girls are excluded either informally or for a fixed period. There has been little research looking at the experiences and specific needs of girls who are unhappy with their education.

bad. I did all sorts of things: wore my uniform all wrong, let off stink bombs, got into fights. I was very loud, I bunked off and started seeing boys and I had the attitude that nobody was going to tell me what to do.

Q Did your parents intervene at this point?

A My dad had started an affair with a family friend and he and my mum were separating. So there was no united front and they found it harder than ever to discipline me. The school

said they wouldn't keep me if I didn't change my attitude. I wasn't going to do that, so I was thrown out. But I knew my mum was unhappy about what was going on with me because she left school at 16 and, although she has been very successful, I think she wanted something more reliable for me. She wanted me to go to university and get a degree.

Q So where did you go to school then?

A I came back to London and went to an international school in

> *" ... A lot of the time I was falling asleep in class from the after-affects of smoking [cannabis] ..."*

West London. It was a very informal school and there were some teachers I got close to, but I started to get involved with drugs at this time. Between classes I went out of school and met up with people, some from other schools, most older than me, who were using drugs. I was smoking cannabis every day and I began experimenting with acid [LSD], ecstasy and speed. It was the best way I could find to deal with the pain of my parents' separation.

Q What effect did this have on you?

A A lot of the time I was falling asleep in class from the after-effects of smoking cannabis and from using up a lot of energy when I was high on ecstasy and speed. When I was awake I was noisy and disruptive. I think my dad got called in because they were worried about how tired I seemed.

Q Did your dad do anything?

A Not that I remember, but one of the teachers I was close to took me aside. He told me that this wasn't the right school for me and that the kids I was hanging out with weren't good for me. He said, if I went on as I was, I'd get kicked out anyway. I was also discovering my sexual power over boys and was very manipulative. I saw it as a way of getting love although, in the end, it turned out to be just a game, or boys wanting sex and nothing else.

Q So did you leave that school?

A Yes, and then my parents sent me to a child psychologist who did tests and recommended a boarding school. This school seemed very liberal and was focussed on drama, but they did random drug tests and searched through the clothes in your drawers. The environment freaked me out. Looking back I think my behaviour had been a desperate attempt to get my parents' attention.

Q As you always managed to get by academically, why didn't you decide to settle down until you could leave?

A Education had no meaning for me. I was very worried and

It's a Fact that...

It's estimated that in the UK around 15 per cent of 11-year-olds and 60 per cent of 15-year-olds have been offered drugs in the last year.

unhappy about the way my life seemed to have been turned upside down, and acting out was a way of not having to feel the pain. My dad, who had promised me he loved Mum and was not leaving, had now left to go and live with his lover. Having my trust in him broken was a very big issue for me.

" ... I think my behaviour had been a desperate attempt to get my parents' attention. "

23

A When I went home from this boarding school at weekends I always wanted to stay until Monday morning and I think Mum, whom I lived with, must have known I was unhappy. But she was having to deal with her own feelings.

Q Did you use drugs at this school?

A I managed to go six months not using and I felt a sense of achievement, but then I went out one weekend and met up with friends and I got right back into

" ... suddenly I realised I had the thing I'd wanted – I was out of school. "

24

the drugs. They did a drug test on me at school and it came up positive showing marijuana and ecstasy. They excluded me on the spot. I was given two hours to get off the school premises.

Q Did that worry you?

A In the cab going home I was crying because I was frightened of the trouble I'd be in. But then suddenly I realised I had the thing I'd wanted - I was out of school. And, in fact, Mum was quite chilled about it. I think she realised school wasn't for me. She told me to go and get a job. I was thrilled because it meant I had independence. I worked for an internet company, but it was the loneliest time I'd known. I went into a six-month depression, I felt very isolated and I was still doing drugs.

Q Was all this because you didn't get much attention from your parents during childhood?

A I think it was and part of that was having two

It's a Fact that...

Children who have been excluded from school are 90 times more likely to end up living on the streets than those who stay on and pass exams. More than a quarter of all children living rough have been excluded from school and 62% have no educational qualifications.

abortions by the time I was 20. So I was very lucky to meet the man I am with now. He's older than me and he has helped me to feel good about myself. Without him I

doubt I'd have had the confidence to write my book* (particularly as I don't have much formal education!) or start my groups for other teenagers who have problems. ∎

Talking Points

◆ One of Jessica's exclusions was because of a positive test for drugs. Should this be grounds for exclusion? Under what circumstances? What if she had taken the drugs off the school premises?

◆ In the end Jessica's mother permits her to leave education and Jessica is pleased because school is 'not for her'. Do you think everyone should be educated to the age of 16? Should children be allowed to stop education if it is not for them? Is a good education necessary for success in life?

* Jessica's book *Sisters Unlimited* is published by Vermilion.

It Happened to Barney

Barney, 12, had four temporary exclusions from secondary school in London before the headteacher and his parents decided he should leave. His mother, Julia, is angry that his special needs, identified after he left, were not recognised by the school and that he did not get the help he needed. Together they describe the experience.

Q How did you like primary school?

A (Barney) It was fine in the beginning and I got on okay. Lessons were easy and I had friends.

A (Julia) Things seemed fine when he started at primary school but there were three changes of headteacher during Barney's time and that meant there wasn't a strong school ethos.

Photographs in this section are posed by models.

Q Did you get on all right the whole time?

A (B) Sometimes I didn't find things easy and some of the children weren't so nice. But the teachers were okay. They didn't hate me like they did in my next school.

A (J) Barney was actually bullied at primary school. Other children picked up his vulnerability and that made him a target for bullying. He dealt with that by being difficult in class and showing off, which is typical for children who can't cope very well.

Q Did you stay at this primary school until you were ready for secondary school?

A (B) Yes, and I felt all right there.

A (J) He was on stage three in the code of conduct for special needs the whole time he was at primary school, which means they were aware he had behavioural difficulties and needed

It's a Fact that...

In Britain children with special educational needs run the highest risk of exclusion - they are excluded at eight times the rate for other youngsters.

support. I didn't know it meant that he should have seen an educational psychologist and he never did. So although the school kept him until the end, and one teacher particularly was very good with him, I felt he was quite unhappy by the time he left. He was getting into trouble regularly and he was quite difficult for the school to manage.

Q Did the school have any ideas why Barney was like this?

A (J) They decided his problems were social not educational so he got visits at school from the local authority welfare department and they were keen to refer us for family therapy. We tried that for a bit but it didn't sort out Barney's behavioural difficulties.

Q So what happened when it was time to leave primary school?

A (B) We went to see two private and two state schools and we chose one of the state ones. I was happy about it because it felt friendly when I visited and the children were nice to me and there was a big playground.

A (J). The school he went to wasn't our first choice, but he had learnt very little at primary and couldn't have got into the private schools we would have liked, which had smaller classes. We weren't in the catchment area for the smaller state school I hoped Barney could go to. The school he was able to go to is very large and has quite

> **" ... in lessons I just sat there and, as I was quiet, nobody took any notice of me."**

a lot of children with severe problems so we had real worries about how Barney would manage. Before he started we phoned the school several times to try to talk about Barney's special needs but it was never possible to have a proper discussion.

Q How were things at first?

A (B) People played with me at free time and I made some friends so that was all right. But in lessons I just sat there and, as I was quiet, nobody took any notice of me.

A (J) Barney's father and I were concerned that Barney should get the support he needed. The school had his special needs file from primary school so should have been aware of his problems. We took him to an educational psychologist ourselves because we wanted to be able to give the school the fullest information. She considered he was dyslexic, dyspraxic and had attention deficit disorder (ADD) and she said he must find the classroom very confusing. She thought he should be statemented, but she wasn't sure we'd succeed in that because although she had identified several things wrong none were very serious on their own.

Q When did things start to go wrong?

A (B) I didn't always go to lessons because I couldn't understand and at first nobody took any notice and I didn't think they cared. Then they put me on report and teachers had to fill in a sheet of paper saying how I had behaved. I got caught forging teachers' signatures and told not to do it again. I was being ticked off for a lot of things and I didn't really know why.

A (J) We became increasingly worried that nobody seemed to be understanding Barney's difficulties. Dyspraxic children tend to have clumsy

It's a Fact that....

Exclusion is very costly, usually more so than keeping a child in full-time education. Factors include the cost of:
◆ health services;
◆ social services;
◆ the criminal justice system (if an excluded child becomes involved in crime);
◆ educational cost.

communication skills and a tremendous dislike of being crowded. It was in this situation that Barney got into the trouble that got him excluded the first time. It was less than a month into the term and Barney was supposed to go swimming. He was excited about this and greeted the PE teacher with great enthusiasm, jumping up and patting him on the head - another thing dyspraxic kids do is overwhelm people they see as being friendly to them. What he did was seen as disrespectful by the teacher and Barney was told he couldn't go swimming after all. He was very upset so then a different teacher said he could go swimming and to get in line. At this point the two teachers started arguing about whether Barney could or couldn't go and he got very upset. Two people tried to calm him and one got kicked on the leg. At this point I was telephoned and asked to collect Barney because he had 'assaulted' a teacher.

I went to the school immediately taking with

Some children are educated at home following exclusion.

me the educational psychologist's report that had just arrived. I gave it to the assistant head who said they were unaware he had any special needs requirements. I was told

> " I was being ticked off for a lot of things and I didn't really know why."

> **" The [school] was just too big and pressurised [for Barney]. He wasn't learning anything..."**

to take Barney home because he was excluded for that day and that he would be internally excluded - this means he spends the day with a member of staff in school - the next day.

Q Did you settle down after that?

A (B) I did go to classes but after a few weeks I

didn't even pick up my pencil because nobody minded if I learnt or not. I found it very boring. I got into trouble again. I was sent home and then excluded in the school for two days.

A (J) Barney was accused by a dinner lady of pushing in the queue but what she probably didn't realise is that he is

30

rarely still because of his ADD. It escalated into nastiness and Barney was very rude to the dinner lady and then to a teacher who said offensive things to him. I was called to a meeting at the school next day and by this time they had read the psychologist's report and it was agreed that there should be a note in Barney's diary that if he got into a state of frustration he could be sent to one of three teachers who would help to calm him down.

Q So did this help?

A (B) I had a best teacher who helped me when I got angry and he let me tell him the things that seemed unfair - when I was picked on by teachers for being bad even though other children were breaking the rules. But then I got excluded again for taking a few swigs of beer that another boy offered me. This time I was excluded and sent home and Mum and Dad were very cross with me.

A (J) We knew Barney was being very disruptive at school and some of the

It's a Fact that...

In the UK only 15 per cent of children who are permanently excluded re-enter mainstream education.

teachers genuinely wanted to help him but didn't have the skills. The place was just too big and pressurised. He wasn't learning anything although he's actually quite bright, but again he was getting attention and trying to buy friendship by being the class clown.

Q Why did you get excluded again?

A (B) I took some fire crackers to school and also some stink bombs and I gave them to people who used them. But when they were caught they told on me so the headteacher knew I had brought them to school. This time I was excluded for four days at home and I really got ticked off by my parents.

A (J) In fact Barney had been excluded another time for getting into conflict with a teacher and then was excluded for a week this time. Barney's dad and I realised his behaviour was a problem for the school. They didn't seem to be able to find any effective way to support his difficulties. We were desperate as we watched our son became more and more unhappy. He lost all confidence and had a total personality shut down.

Q How did you feel about school, Barney?

A (B) I didn't like going and I thought the teachers all wanted me to leave.

31

A (J) All this happened during the first term he was at secondary school and his dad and I realised we had to get him out before things got any worse.

Q So how did you feel about this?

A (B) I was glad because although I missed my friends I didn't want to go on getting into trouble there.

A (J) Once we had decided Barney should leave we went to the educational psychologist again because we wanted to try to get him statemented so that the local education authority would take responsibility for his special needs. I had asked the secondary

" The change in Barney is like a miracle."

school to help us get him statemented before but nothing happened. We then looked for a new school and found Fairley House, which specialises in teaching special needs' children. They had Barney for a three-day trial and then agreed to take him. Just before he started he got his statement, so we get support from the local authority for this school.

Q How do you feel about this new school?

A (B) I am really happy. I don't know how but they have helped me and I am doing lots of work. I have a book for handwriting. The teachers praise me when I do well.

A (J) The change in Barney is like a miracle. He is in small, very focussed learning groups and the school thinks he's doing really well. He's following a normal curriculum and he won a cup for his IT [Information Technology] work. He is getting occupational therapy to help deal with his frustrations. The wonderful thing is we can see he is happy. He's returned to his true personality and he's gaining trust again, having felt that teachers were his enemies. But he hasn't forgotten the feeling of being excluded. I think if his needs had been picked up at primary school and he'd been statemented, something could have been done. Now the aim is to get him back into the mainstream but only when he can really cope. ■

> "I think if his needs had been picked up at primary school and he'd been statemented, something could have been done."

Talking Points

◆ Having special needs is not an officially acceptable reason for exclusion. However if a school does not have the resources to cope with a particular special needs child, do you think they should be able to exclude? What if they believe the pupil would be better off in a special school?

◆ What do you think any school should learn from this experience?

◆ Barney is progressing and is happy at his special needs school. Why do you think his parents want him to go back into mainstream education eventually?

It Happened to Mustapha

Mustapha, a mature, intelligent 17-year-old, lives with his Muslim family in Melbourne. He plans to become a doctor and is set to go to university at the end of his final year at a state run school in Melbourne. When Mustapha was 15 he was excluded from a private Muslim school where his mother was teaching. He says the exclusion altered the direction of his entire life.

Q You have an unusual background. Can you explain a little?

A I was born in London. My mother is English and my father is from Pakistan. I was six when we came to Australia.

Q What was it like at your old school?

A It was a private Muslim college. I was there for about five years. I was bullied all through school because my mum was a teacher. They picked on me all the time. My mum was well-known for giving detention - and they took it out on me.

Q Describe yourself at the time.

A I was left out of everything, I didn't have any friends. I was just there by myself. I guess I was what they'd call a nerd, stuck by myself. I couldn't play sport - no one would choose me. I was always left on the side. I felt like an outcast.

Q Can you recall the moment when you were told you were excluded?

A Yes - I was in class and the vice-principal teacher came in and told me to clear out my locker. It was the most embarrassing moment of my life.

Q Why were you excluded?

A I was in year 8 and they skipped me up to year 10. I got the highest marks in year 8 and in year 10. I made friends with a couple of boys in my class who were known as hackers. I got a false sense of friendship from these boys.

> " ... I didn't have any friends. I was just there by myself."

It's a Fact that...

Across Australian states there are a number of terms used to describe a student's removal from school, including suspension (short and long), in-school suspension expulsion, exclusion and prohibition from enrolment. This can be confusing both for children and parents.

What happened was that they asked me to get a disk so I brought in a disk and they did something on the computers that I didn't know about. They blamed it all on me because the disk was one of my mother's.

Q Can you explain in more detail?

A They saved something onto the disk and were caught cheating. They had exam papers in their lockers. They blamed it all back on me and I had nothing to prove that it wasn't me because the disk belonged to my mother. It actually had her name on it in her handwriting. It was the perfect alibi.

Q What exactly were you accused of?

A Of taking Year 11 History papers - a subject I wasn't even doing. They thought I'd taken the papers and given them to my friends, but it made no sense.

Q Did anyone believe you were innocent?

A None of the teachers. They gave me no support.

Q Can you think why?

A I don't know. I just don't know. But the school was a really hardline school, as religious schools can be. It could have been

> ## "[My father] believed I didn't do it - and he still wants to prove that I'm innocent."

because teachers set higher standards for the children of other teachers. So it makes it worse - they look down on you if you're accused of something.

Q Did people see you as a troublemaker?

A I don't know how to say this, but I'm a very physically weak, peaceful person. I don't have the strength to fight with people. I keep to myself.

Q How did the other students react?

A They thought I had done it and they said things like, 'Oh, good job!' They were all happy about it!

Q Can you remember how you felt when all this was happening?

A I was at the brink. You know, everything is collapsing down on you. You're finished. But it wasn't like that afterwards. I realise that you're never finished and good things can happen later.

Q How did your family react when they knew you were excluded?

A My father was terribly disappointed. He believed I didn't do it - and he still wants to prove that I'm innocent. We will do something, but after I finish this year. My family

gave me a lot of support at the time. It was hard for them as well.

Q What was the worst thing?

A The humiliation. My family didn't put pressure on me but the community does. They look at you and say, 'Oh, that person is a cheat.' That's very hard for my family too.

Q Was there anyone who disappointed you?

A Oh, yes, one of my best teachers, the teacher who was closest to me, the one who actually taught History and was also the English teacher. I would have thought that he'd have

It's a Fact that...

An Australian survey of excluded children revealed:

◆ 45 per cent were not told of their rights,
◆ 45 per cent were not given information about how the exclusion could be challenged,
◆ 44 per cent were not given a hearing or meeting at which they could put their point of view, neither were their parents,
◆ 44 per cent did not think the decision was fair.

believed me but he didn't. Whenever we had the interviews in the principal's office he was there and I didn't have any sense that he was with me.

Q What strategies did you use to move on?

A I changed everything about myself - my whole personality. How can I explain? I just started questioning my own idea of myself. Overnight I changed everything about myself - the way I dressed, the way I talked to my friends, all the things I did.

Q Why did you change the way you dressed?

A Oh, I was a total nerd! That's the best description. I changed the way I dressed to fit in with the people I stick around with. I used to be different because I wasn't interested in clothes and the way I looked. So I stood out from the rest. Now I look like everyone else. I blend in and you can't tell the difference between me and everyone else. The only difference is my test mark!

Q Where do you go to school now?

A A state school. I'm in Year 12, the final year. I've been there for two years.

"Overnight I changed everything about myself..."

37

Q Was it difficult to go back to school?

A The exclusion ruined my reputation because it was on my reports. I was lucky to get into the new school because no other school would look at me - even the state schools. So I was lucky to get in here.

Q How have you changed since moving schools and going through this trauma of exclusion?

A I've become more confident in myself and I've met people I would say were real friends. I've developed because of this. I've started debating and that gives me some confidence. Debating is really good for people like me.

" The exclusion ruined my reputation because it was on my reports. "

It's a Fact that...

There is no clear legal requirement in Australia or New Zealand that a pupil excluded from school be provided with alternative educational opportunities.

More than 40 per cent of the queries received by the Australian National Children's and Youth Law Centre in 1999 and 2000 relating to school exclusions were complaints of unfair processes in non-government schools.

> ## "It was one of the best things that ever happened to me. It changed my life."

Q So it has been a positive or even a good experience?

A I'm a different person. I'm happy. It was perfect for me. If I hadn't left the school I would have been that same person. It was one of the best things that ever happened to me. It changed my life. I'm a better person than I was. I'm stronger. When the worst has happened you know you can face anything. I don't need to worry about things. I've gotten over it.

Q Do you think this would have happened differently if you had been at a state school before?

A I think private schools put too much pressure on you.

It's better for a student to be at a state school and even better if the parent isn't teaching there! State schools are more accepting. It's more diverse. In Islamic schools there tends to be less of a mix so it is harder to fit in.

Q What do you want to do with your life?

A I want to be a doctor and I want to do that because I want to be better than my dad. He's a

dentist. He wants me to be a doctor.

Q What would your advice be to other people in your situation?

A Not to worry about it. Try not to think too much about it and move on as fast as you can. If you're a good student, stick with people you can trust and don't mix with the worst people in the class, don't try to impress other people and just be who you are. ∎

Talking Points

◆ Mustapha found a new school to attend, but it was difficult because the exclusion was on his record. Do you think it is fair for exclusion to be such a stigma? Should it be removed from school records? In what circumstances?

◆ Two years on, Mustapha's father still wants to prove his son's innocence. Do you think this is a good idea? What would you want to do in Mustapha's position?

◆ Mustapha changed the way he dresses in order to blend in and be 'normal'. Was it necessary to go this far? What do you think is more important - to fit in with other people, or to be yourself?

It Happened to Gary

Gary is headteacher at Eveline Lowe primary school in East London. He explains why he sometimes has to exclude pupils.

Q Yours is an inner city school. Do you have many children with challenging behaviour and problems that make them difficult to handle?

A I think any school in an area with social deprivation and where there is a lot of unemployment has a lot of stresses to cope with, and anger overflows easily. Where children may not get enough attention, or the wrong kind, they will have some issues and problems. And we certainly do. There are times when the children are very challenging.

Q So do you see exclusion as an important measure for keeping discipline in your school?

A It's important to be able to exclude if it is absolutely necessary for the good of everyone else in the school,

It's a Fact that...

All councils in the UK are required to provide full-time mainstream education for pupils within 20 days of exclusion, or provide 25 hours tuition per week until it is found.

but I work very hard to avoid having to do it.

Q Are all exclusions the same?

A No. There are two kinds of exclusion. Fixed-term exclusion, which is for a limited time, is to tell the child their behaviour will not be tolerated, but at the same time to let them know they will be taken back if they are willing to change their behaviour. The other is permanent exclusion where you have probably already temporarily excluded them and the child continues to behave just as badly.

Q What is your school like?

A My starting point for the school is not discipline but creating an atmosphere where children feel good, where their individuality can be developed and where there is a lot of focus on helping them develop good relationships and care for each other. To do this you need staff who really enjoy children and want to treat them well and do not try to assert authority by shouting at them, belittling them and frightening them - as certainly does happen in some schools. At the same time I have high expectations of the children, and expect them to behave well too. But most children, if they come into a place that is calm and respectful, will behave that way themselves.

Q But not all?

A There are always a few children whose lives are so chaotic, who see everyone as being against them, who are damaged in whatever way, that they cannot seem to control their behaviour and, as I said, I have a bottom line for what will be tolerated from them.

Q So what is the bottom line?

A I will not tolerate violence, assault, injury, fighting. I don't want children coming to school frightened because they may be bullied, victimised or suffer from another child's bad behaviour. Nor will I put up with violence towards the staff. I am also tough about disruptive behaviour if it goes on and on and means the teacher uses a great deal of time and energy on one child so that the others don't get the education they need and deserve.

" ... I work very hard to avoid having to [exclude]. "

> **" I don't want children coming to school frightened because they may be bullied, victimised or suffer from another child's bad behaviour."**

Q Is there a process leading up to exclusion?

A There are a number of things I do to try to get the child to change their behaviour before I exclude. We all see it as a last resort at this school.

Q So, typically, what happens?

A The teacher will talk with the child first and try to find out if there is something troubling him or her. Then if bad behaviour is going on in class, they might be sent out for a while and it can be for quite a long time if they are really troublesome. Children don't like that because on the whole lessons are fun in our school. For aggressive and violent behaviour and disruptiveness in class that doesn't stop, a child would be sent to the deputy head or to me for a one-to-one talk. We really do try to understand why they feel the need to behave the way they do.

Q What is the role of parents here?

A The next thing would be to call the parents in and ask if we have their backing in using sanctions against their child, and to see what they think about his or her behaviour. Obviously we need parents to support us. Those parents who can't grasp that we won't tolerate what is going on will give their children very negative messages. This makes it much harder for their child to settle down. For instance I had a parent who said to their child, 'Hit anyone back who hits you and don't tolerate teachers shouting at you; you show them.'

Q So parents are an important part of what happens?

A When parents won't support us - and happily it's very much the exception - we tell them there's no alternative but to exclude their child formally. They then do not have the right to send their child to the school unless they and their child will opt into our code of conduct. The point I stress is that it's their choice.

It's a Fact that...

In 1999 schools in England and Wales excluded ten times more children than in Northern Ireland and four times more than in Scotland.

" We really do try to understand why they feel the need to behave the way they are."

" ... I have to protect my staff who may also be attacked and abused by children we have to exclude. "

Q Do you always carry through the threat to exclude?

A I do. It's no use saying you will do something and not going through with it. So often, these are the children who have no consistency in their lives, with empty threats of punishments being made and not carried all the way through.

Q How long do you exclude the child the first time?

A There's no fixed rule on this. It could be a day, a week or longer, whatever is appropriate. But if the child comes back to school and nothing has improved then it will be permanent exclusion.

Q But in the end isn't it failing a child who may well be aggressive and disruptive because they have such problems of their own?

A I wish we were equipped to help very damaged children but we aren't; and in the end I have to think about what is good for all the pupils in the school. We have some very fragile, very needy children who can be made very unhappy indeed if they are intimidated and terrified when they come here and feel nobody will protect them. And I have to protect my staff who may also be attacked and abused by children we have to exclude.

It's a Fact that...

Schools that exclude few pupils tend to be better at managing behaviour than those that exclude a lot of pupils.

Q How does it feel as headteacher when you have to exclude?

A It always feels like a failure and happily I have not had to exclude a child for a while now. I believe that if you make a school a place where children feel cared for, even those who come with a reputation for bad behaviour will calm down. ■

Talking Points

◆ Much of the decision to exclude a child at this school depends on the support, or lack of support, from their parents. Is this fair? Should a child who perhaps gets a raw deal at home, also lose out on their education?

◆ Read Mustapha's interview on page 34. How do you think he would have been treated at this school? What may have helped him?

◆ What guidelines do you think schools should follow before an exclusion is imposed?

Useful addresses and contacts

UNITED KINGDOM
Local council education department numbers are listed in telephone directories.

Department for Education and Skills (DfES)
Provides detailed guidance on exclusion on their website:
www.dfes.org.uk

The Children's Society
A society that works with government and other professionals to research and advise on key issues of concern to benefit children.

Edward Rudolf House, Margery Street
London, WC1X OJL
020 7841 4400
www.the-childrens-society.org.uk

The Advisory Centre for Education (ACE)
An independent advice centre for parents in England and Wales, offering advice about state education, including exclusion.

1c Aberdeen Studios, 22 Highbury Grove
London N5 2DQ
Exclusion line: 020 7704 9822
www.ace-ed.org.uk

The Who Cares? Trust
A national charity offering advice and support, to children and young people in care or foster homes.

Kemp House, 152-160 City Road
London EC1V 2NP
Helpline: 0500 564570
www.thewhocarestrust.org.uk

The Children's Legal Centre
A national charity dealing with the law and how it affects young people.

University of Essex
Wivenhoe Park
Colchester
Essex C04 3SQ
Advice line: 01206 873 820
www.childrenslegalcentre.com

Education Otherwise
A UK-based membership organisation that provides support for families whose children are being educated outside school.

Helpline: 0870 7300074
www.education-otherwise.org

AUSTRALIA AND NEW ZEALAND
Human Rights and Equal Opportunites Commission
A website that includes information about children and education:

www.hreoc.gov.au/human_rights/children/seen_and_heard

Australian National Children's and Youth Law Centre
Provides guidelines on the law for under 18s, across all states. The website contains advice and contact details:

www.lawstuff.org.au

Youth Law in New Zealand
Provides free legal advice for children and young people up to the age of 25.

PO Box 7657 Wellesley Street
www.youthlaw.co.nz

Glossary

amphetamine (speed)
A drug that increases energy.

attention deficit disorder (ADD)
The main features of this disorder are: a lack of sustained attention to tasks, impulsiveness and being very physically restless.

cannabis
A drug which is smoked or eaten.

crack cocaine
A very strong form of the drug cocaine.

dyslexia
A disorder that causes learning difficulty in reading, spelling or numeracy. It is sometimes called 'word blindness'.

dyspraxia
A disorder which affects sufferer's brains. It is associated with problems of movement, language and thought. It affects the planning of what to do and how to do it.

ecstasy
A drug that increases energy and can cause the user to see things that are not actually there.

ethos
The individual spirit or attitude of a place.

exclusion
Exclusion is when a child is sent home from school as a punishment, or because he or she is thought to be unmanageable. It may be temporary (a few days or more) or permanent, which means that the child will have to find alternative education. It is sometimes called expulsion or suspension.

hacker
A person who gains access to computer data, usually without permission.

hardline school
A school with strict rules.

liberal school
A liberal school has less strict rules.

LSD (acid)
A powerful drug that causes people to see things that are not actually there.

NVQ (National Vocational Qualification)
A recognised attainment in a practical skill such as building or carpentry.

private school
A school that is managed by a private body and is usually funded by fee-paying students.

psychologist
Someone who studies people's minds in order to help them. An educational psychologist is specially trained to understand school children.

rehabilitate
To help someone lead a normal life through education or training.

speed
A type of amphetamine.

statement (of special needs)
A child who is statemented for special needs has been given official recognition of their problems. This means they will be given more educational support.

state school
A school that is maintained by the state and attendance is free.

Urdu
An official language of Pakistan and India, which is also spoken throughout the world.

vulnerable
someone who is easily upset or harmed.

Index

e...
th...

Viol...
disru...
truan...
relatio...

Then dis...

In groups:
One person...
this book. Th...
should not ho...
then it is put t...

48

Glossary

amphetamine (speed)
A drug that increases energy.

attention deficit disorder (ADD)
The main features of this disorder are: a lack of sustained attention to tasks, impulsiveness and being very physically restless.

cannabis
A drug which is smoked or eaten.

crack cocaine
A very strong form of the drug cocaine.

dyslexia
A disorder that causes learning difficulty in reading, spelling or numeracy. It is sometimes called 'word blindness'.

dyspraxia
A disorder which affects sufferer's brains. It is associated with problems of movement, language and thought. It affects the planning of what to do and how to do it.

ecstasy
A drug that increases energy and can cause the user to see things that are not actually there.

ethos
The individual spirit or attitude of a place

exclusion
Exclusion is where a child is sent home from school as a punishment, or because he or she is thought to be unmanageable. It may be temporary (a few days or more) or permanent, which means that the child will have to find alternative education. It is sometimes called expulsion or suspension.

hacker
A person who gains access to computer data, usually without permission.

hardline school
A school with strict rules.

liberal school
A liberal school has less strict rules.

LSD (acid)
A powerful drug that causes people to see things that are not actually there.

NVQ (National Vocational Qualification)
A recognised attainment in a practical skill, such as building or carpentry.

private school
A school that is managed by a private body and is usually funded by fee-paying students.

psychologist
Someone who studies people's minds in order to help them. An educational psychologist is specially trained to understand school children.

rehabilitate
To help someone lead a normal life through education or training.

speed
A type of amphetamine.

statement (of special needs)
A child who is statemented for special needs has been given official recognition of their problems. This means they will be given more educational support.

state school
A school that is maintained by the state and attendance is free.

Urdu
An official language of Pakistan and India, which is also spoken throughout the world.

vulnerable
someone who is easily upset or harmed.

Index

Getting active!

On your own:
'Permanent exclusion is never the right answer.' Write a short piece explaining whether you agree or disagree with this statement. Where you can bring in example from the interviews in this book.

In pairs:
Make three lists: 'permanent exclusion', 'temporary exclusion', 'no exclusion', and put the following offences under which heading you think the offence warrants:

Violent behaviour, repeatedly not wearing school uniform, drug-taking, disruptive classroom behaviour, threatening a teacher, cheating on a test, truancy, racist behaviour, bullying, stealing from other pupils, bad relationship with teacher, pregnancy.

Then discuss your reasons with another pair.

In groups:
One person takes on the role of one of the excluded pupils interviewed in this book. They should put together an argument to explain why they should not have been excluded. Another person argues against them – then it is put to the audience to vote.